Old Scarborough
Photo Archive

Acknowledgements

Thanks are due to the following, from whose articles, text or photographs have been used - in some cases by internet download. We have tried to acknowledge all extracts below but if any copyright holders have been missed please advise the publisher and a correction will be made in future editions.

Colin Hinson; Len Gazzard; Stephen Craven; Marie Jaques; Janet Hardisty; Brian Shaw; Jeff Allinson; David Jackson; Pauline Allen; Chris Jones; Fatima Hey; Tim Lawson; Barry McAvoy; Daniel Taylor; David Impey; Howard Johnson; Clive Fattorini; The Late Roy Child.

Contents

Shops And Hotels

Borough Of Scarborough Information Centre on St Nicholas Street opposite the Town Hall.

Victoria Cafe in 1980.

Bakery at 10 Westborough.

W. Vasey in Ramshill, now Trevor Wharton Carpets.

Rawling & Co. rock making exhibition on the Foreshore.

Roseberry Avenue adjoining Seamer Road.

Ashley's Spa Boarding Establishment now Palm Court Hotel.

Electrodec on Victoria Road.

Corner of Seamer Road into Falsgrave showing a row
of shops and the White Horse Pub.

Land & Co's Family Cash Supply Stores on South Street.

Westborough in 1897.

Shop on the corner of Sandside and Eastborough.

Charles Smith's shop on St Johns Road.

CO-OP on the corner of Franklin Street in the early 1920's.

Greenlays Pork Shop on Bar Street not long before closing.

A view down Westborough with Burwells on the corner of Vernon Place.

Looking down the town with Debenhams on the right and Dixons just in view on the left.

The famous Rowntrees/Debenhams department store in Westborough in the early 1980's.

William Rowntree owned and operated various businesses in Scarborough, He had a drapers and hatters shop at the old town hall on St Nicholas Street, a furniture shop at 41 and 43 Newborough plus warehouses and showrooms at 5 and 6 Market Street. By 1875 his three sons were partners in the firm.

W.Rowntree and sons were well known, and was the place to buy luxurious and expensive goods usually by the wealthy.
Every part of the business was soaring and ready for expansion. William started to look for a site which would be big enough for him to erect a new building that would accommodate all his shops, and so in 1879 he bought 38 - 40 Westborough.

The following year he bought the adjoining properties 33 - 37 but sold number 40 to a local butcher.
He then decided to build at the corner of Westborough and York Place, a department store that the North East had never seen.

The new Rowntrees building's foundation stone was laid on 7th July 1881, the architect was Edward Burgess of London, the cost of the build was £30,000.
The building had four storey's and a 112 ft frontage onto Westborough, at each end of the building were towers one an octagonal and the other a square.

On the front of the store had large display windows, seven of which had 11 ft square sheets of glass while the frames were made from oak and above these were beautiful stone carvings. There were three entrances to the store, the largest one near York Place. The ground floor had three departments, from the largest entrance you entered into the carpet and upholstery department. Then from the centre entrance was the drapery and dress department, the smallest department was the gentlemen's outfitters. Above this part of the building were workrooms, on the second floor a private residence and on the third were accommodation for resident employees. There were 2 oak panelled staircases, the larger of the two went up from the carpet and upholstery department to the first floor where it had 12 ft windows on each side. This floor sold and displayed furniture for dining rooms and sitting rooms.

On the second and third floor was bedroom furniture bedsteads and bedding, again this was bright due to the huge windows and the well that went up through all the floors and connected to a glass skylight.
Rowntrees was the first place in Scarborough to have electric light, the power came from two dynamo machines driven by a gas engine set in concrete in the basement. The basement had all the walls covered in wood to keep out damp. The store had a lift, not for customer use but for moving stock only, until the end of the 1800's when they got a hydraulic one and a male member of staff would take customers to each floor.
In December 1972 Debenhams bought out Rowntrees but continued to use the Rowntrees name until 1982 when the name disappeared from the front replaced by Debenhams.

The store remained in use till 1990 when the opening phase of the Brunswick Pavilion shopping centre brought a new Debenhams. The old store next door was demolished to make way for the rest of the Brunswick development.

The Bull Hotel (1896) Opened in 1869, later renamed "The Balmoral Hotel".

The Balmoral Centre now stands where The Balmoral Hotel once was.

A view of the town centre showing the Huntsman Hotel and The Balmoral Hotel next door.

Westborough with Marks and Spencer just visible behind the bus.

Westborough viewed from the end of Aberdeen Walk in the 1960's.

Woolworths in Westborough adjoining Vernon Road.

A view looking up Westborough in 1980 with Woolworths shop
sign just visible to the left.

The corner of York Place adjoining Westborough.

St Thomas Street viewed from St Nicholas Street with Cooplands on the right.

Marie Jaques shop in Victoria Road during Benelux Festival week.

Boots in St Nicholas Street, now Lloyds Bank.

Trams in the Town Centre with Tonks on the right.

J. Tonks & Sons (104 & 105)Westborough.

Joseph Tonks the first, after serving and completing his time in the army, he learned his craft as a ship's carpenter with Tindalls in Scarborough.

Being adventurous he then joined the Merchant Navy sailing to Spain with stores for the troops fighting against Napoleon. Once his Navy service had finished he returned again to Scarborough and started a cabinet making business in King Street.

In 1820, when he was 64 years of age, he joined forces with Francis Haigh a cabinet making establishment in Queen Street.

This was the year that the foundation stone of The House of Tonks was laid. Joseph the second, his son, was 11 years old at the time but records show that he was an active member of the firm 10 years later.

Joseph and his son worked together to build up a successful business until Joseph the first died in 1846 aged 90. Joseph the second continued in partnership with Francis Haigh until Francis's death in 1860.

Upholstery and undertaking departments were added to the original cabinet making and John, the son of Joseph the second joined the business. He persuaded his father to move premises to 103 Westborough where it would be in a more prominent position on the main street of the town, he also thought it would be a good place to expand the firm, and so he developed the repository and removal side of the business.

The Westborough premises were rebuilt in 1867 and extended to cover twice their original area in 1890. Their warehouses had become huge and their horse drawn removal vans were well known all over the country.

Tonks & Sons supplied local hotels with their furniture, floor coverings, bedding and furnishings.

In 1876 came the highest accolade of all a Royal warrant from the Prince of Wales, to whom they had supplied goods when he stayed in Yorkshire. The warrant was regranted when the Prince came to throne as Edward VII.

John continued to expand the business and resided at The House of Tonks, personally greeting each customer, employees enjoyed his kindness and felt appreciated.

As a good kind hearted man, it was said that John supported every good cause brought to his attention. He felt responsible for the welfare of his employees and was known to send a sick man on a sea voyage to help with his recovery. There was a story told about a boy who went to work for him and soon after his arrival he accidentally broke a valuable chandelier destined for some Victorian gentleman's castle, in those days an unimaginable disaster. The boy pictured himself not only dismissed but saddled for the rest of his life with the burden of making good the loss. Instead an imposing but kind father figure talked to him, understood how the accident had happened, and gave him another chance. The boy continued working at Tonks till retirement when he left to enjoy a pension from the firm till his death.

By 1902 John had taken four of his Sons into partnership, when John died in 1913 the year of his golden wedding, his sons continued, converting the business into a limited liability company in 1920.

There were improvements and extensions made to the Westborough shop, Warehouses and depositories, one of them being the lift installed at the Westborough shop in 1923, and two years later the premises again were extended by adding the adjoining properties. The premises occupied 3,000 superficial yards of floor area, divided up into 9 showrooms.

The repositories situated in Gladstone Lane had 36 separate lock up rooms besides other strong rooms for valuables.

Tonks was world famous for its goods and services. The store in Westborough had a magnificent staircase and every department you could think of including a green and blue colour themed coffee lounge on the top floor where customers could enjoy the amazing sea view over the roof tops of Scarborough. As a family business it traded for over 160 years all by direct descendants of the man who started it all, until managing director Nigel Tonks sadly closed it's doors in 1980. Today the Superdrug Store and Cooplands shop now stand where The House of Tonks once was.

Old Scarborough Photo Archive

A view of the Spa Bridge looking onto St Nicholas Cliff before
the Grand Hotel.

The Post Office/Shop at Osgodby in 1980.

Friars Way leading to Cross Street in 1930.

Christmas time at Thompsons Butchers on Victoria Road around 1931
with turkeys hanging outside.

Scalby Mills Hotel in the late 1930's.

Scarborough Town "B" Band outside Currys on the corner of
St Thomas Street, now Heron Foods.

Hillards being built on Westwood in the 1980's.

Another photo of Hillards being built.

A view of the Pavilion Hotel, demolished in 1973, with the railway station on the right.

Falsgrave showing a row of shops, the pub on the right is now the
Tap & Spile.

Theatres & Cinemas

The Odeon Cinema on Northway in 1976.

The Royal Opera House on St Thomas Street also in 1976.

Capitol Theatre as Mecca Bingo in 1976.

The Futurist was originally designed by Frank A. Tugwell and was built on the former site of Catlins Arcadia which opened in July 1903 and was closed and demolished in 1920 to make way for the new Futurist cinema.

Work began on the Futurist on 27th August 1920 and it opened on 14th May 1921 as a cinema. The exterior had a beautiful Italian marble appearance. It originally had a capacity of 2,393. In 1957 it was converted into a theatre by Captain Ritson and the stage was extended making its new capacity of 2,155. As well as being altered inside, outside was drastically altered too as in 1968 the architecture was covered in yellow coloured tiles/cladding. Underneath this cladding The Futurists real beauty still exists and some of its original exterior can be seen towards the top of the building.

During the 1980's the Borough Council took over the Futurist and leased it to Apollo Leisure (UK) Ltd until 2002.
Since December 2002 Brenda and Barrie Stead who run the Hollywood Plaza Cinema took over the Futurist.

The Futurist was the 5th largest Theatre in the country outside London and was a very popular place for locals and holidaymaker's a like but it was struggling to survive due to lack of investment. After many locals tried to save the futurist by starting a campaign and a petition unfortunately the Futurist finally closed its doors in January 2014.

The Londesborough Picture House has been demolished and is now a cafe and shops.

Floral Hall built in 1928, demolished 1989, the site is now the Alexandra Bowls Centre.

Aberdeen Walk Picture House.

The Grand Opera House on St Thomas Street.

The Grand Opera House on St Thomas Street, built in 1877 and demolished in 2004.

The popular Floral Hall on a busy day.

Transport

Two buses parked at Northway Bus Station.

A view inside Northway Bus Station.

Here are another two views of Northway Bus Station.

Northway Bus Station before redevelopment.

The bus station in Vine Street.

A view inside Vine Street Bus Station.

Bus station at Westwood now Tesco's.

Another view of Westwood Bus Station.

A Skipper bus on the corner of Albemarle Crescent with the neeb shop on the left.

Trams on Manor Road with sea cadet band to the right
heading towards Wykeham Street.

Tram lines being layed near The Aquarium.

The Great Tram Disaster Of 1925.

THE SOUTH FORESHORE, SCARBOROUGH.

A busy day on the Foreshore with trams and the sea water baths
just visible in the background.

North Marine Road with trams.

Scarborough Railway Station in 1898.

Gallows close, all tracks gone by 1986 and is now Sainsbury's Supermarket.

Applebys seafront service outside the Corner Cafe.

North Eastern Railway Goods Station.

Decorated bicycle competition at the Open Air Theatre in June 1972.

A ticket inspector standing in the middle of the road waiting for a tram in 1923.

Wallace Arnold Tours situated on Columbus Ravine now Care Micro.

Parish's Garage at the Westwood/Somerset Terrace/Valley Bridge Road/
Northway crossroad junction in 1976.

Falsgrave Train Station on Londesborough Road in 1913,
opened in 1908 and closed in 1963.

3 open top buses advertising what were some of Scarborough's best attractions in the 1990's.

Union Jack Motors in Hanover Road.

A busy day in the town centre.

First ration free fuel day after the second world war.

Arundales Car Centre on Northway in the 1990's with the
Shell petrol station just visible on the right.

County Garages on St Thomas Street now Matalan.

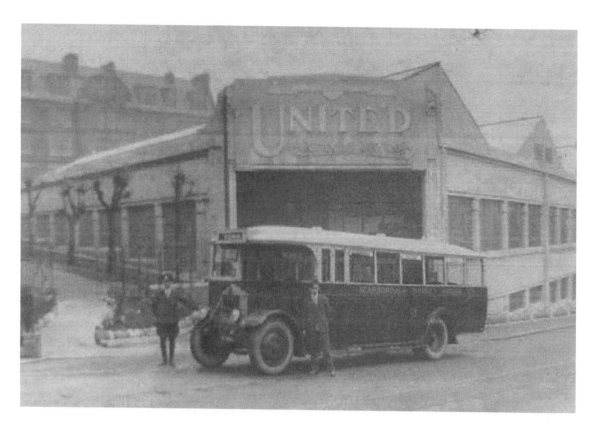

United bus station on Vernon Road in 1929 with a bus outside.

Tram to town next door to Olympia in 1977.

Hospitals

Scarborough hospital when it first opened in 1893 on Friars Entry.

The hospital on Scalby Road, opened in 1936 to replace the
hospital on Friars Entry.

The hospital nurses home, a separate building which had 60 bedrooms as well as sitting rooms, waiting rooms and a kitchen.

A view of a typical nurses bedroom inside the home.

The Royal North Sea Bathing Infirmary on the Foreshore.

Scarborough General Hospital, date unknown.

Attractions

Scalby Mills Amusements.

The chairlift to Mr Marvels from Scalby Mills.

Entrance to Zoo & Marineland.

Flipper and Jenky dolphin show.

Rides at Mr Marvels.

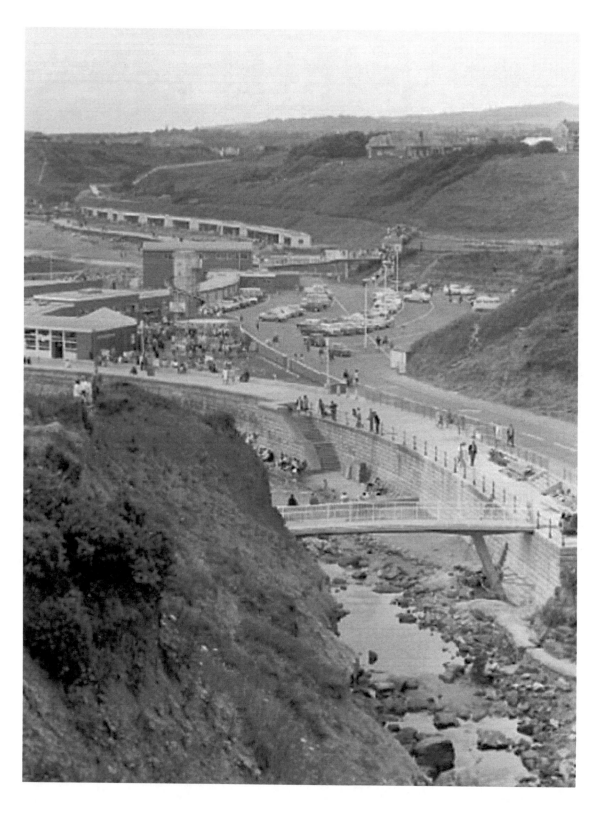

Scalby Mills, date unknown.

Monkey Island at Scalby Mills, removed in the 1960's.

Scalby Mills Hotel.

Thompson's Switchback roller coaster on Royal Albert Drive, opened in 1888 and ceased operating after the storm which destroyed most of the North Bay Pier on 7th January 1905.

The Hispaneola on the mere.

The Windmill Amusements on the Foreshore.

The South Bay Pool after the great storm surge of January 1953.

Bathing Pool and South Bay, Scarborough. "Empire View" 63 42

The South Bay Pool was designed by a local engineer Harry Smith and was opened on the 21st of July 1915 by Mayor and Mayoress Christopher and Maisie Graham.

The pool cost £13,200 to build and held nearly two million gallons of water. There was no high wall around the outer edge of the pool so water from the sea would flood over, after world war 1 the outer wall was heightened and in 1934 a high diving board was installed with a height of 32 ft. The pool measured 330 ft by 165 ft and once was the largest outdoor pool in Europe. It hosted many major swimming events, aqua shows and diving displays.

In the 1970's the south bay pool was popular for school swimming galas. By 1979 the pool was making just £5 a day. The borough council announced in 1980 that the pool would not open as it was losing money and needed expensive repair work. A campaign was launched by various groups and associations to save the South Bay Pool.

Two months later the campaign raised £5000 and the council added £15,000 to keep the pool open for the summer.

In September 1989 sadly the pool was permanently closed. The pool stood derelict for many years and attracted vandals and drug users so the council put up a security fence as a measure to keep out trouble.

After much debate about what to do with the area, in 2001 the borough council revealed plans to spend over £1.1m filling in the pool and in turning it into a star map. By 2003 they had decided to carry out their plan. The star map which is 26m in width still stands today. It shows the 42 brightest stars and major constellations that can be seen from Scarborough.

The circus arriving in town coming up Victoria Road with
Aberdeen Walk on the right.

The Rotunda Museum with horse and cart outside.

Paratrooper ride at the Luna Park.

What was left of the towns only indoor swimming pool, originally part of the Aquarium situated just below the spa bridge, after demolition it was renamed Aquarium Top.

Public Houses

Ye Old No. Eleven in Newborough.

Sandside with The Newcastle Packet in the centre of the photo.

Sandside with The Golden Ball on the right.

The Denmark Arms on St Mary's Walk.

Old Scarborough Photo Archive

Beehive Inn on Sandside.

Miscellaneous

The old post office on Huntriss Row on a sunny day in 1908 before moving to Aberdeen Walk in 1910.

Clarke's Aerated waters and bottling Co. Ltd.

The business was founded in 1889 by Richard Clarke at 19 North Street.

The factory shown above was situated in Clifton Street, Scarborough, opposite Aberdeen Walk and was practically in the centre of town.

The factory was especially built for the purpose of manufacturing mineral waters in the year 1900 and covered an area of approx 8,000 square feet.

The whole of the ground floor was covered with modern machinery used in the manufacturing of soft drinks, together with the boiler house. The first floor was utilised for the manufacturing of fruit syrups, juices and squashes, whilst the second floor was used for storage and the works canteen.

Another photo showing part of the storage room for soft drinks which had a capacity to store over 10,000 dozens. Modern conveyors minimise the handling of the finished goods from the factory to the store and from the store to the lorries for delivery.

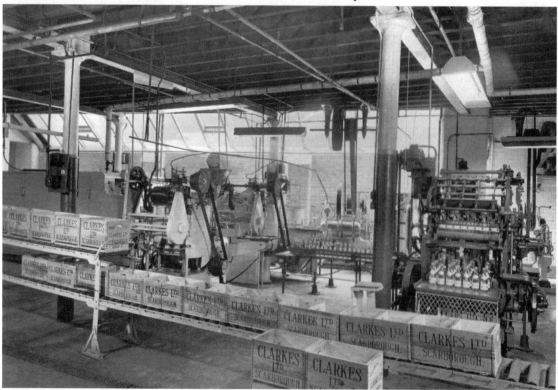

Part of the modern machinery used for the washing and filling of mineral waters. The machines shown in the photograph above wash, fill, crown and label the bottles. The labelling machine on the right would put two labels on each bottle at the rate of 4,800 bottles per hour.

All bottles passed through the washing machine and were first rinsed with cold water. They were then rinsed 3 times with warm water. They then passed through to the proper cleansing part of the machine, where they were subjected to hot rinses of detergent with powerful jets of a solution at 160 degrees. After this, they are again rinsed with warm water and then finally with cold water. Result :- A perfectly clean, brilliant, sterile bottle.

This photograph shows part of the syrup room where the various concentrates were made. It contained numerous glass lined tanks, mixing machines and the water filtration plant. Every care was taken to ensure the raw materials used were of the best quality and that the resulting beverages lived up to the high standards set by Clarke's for over 70 years.

This photograph shows Clarke's fleet of lorries which enabled them to give an efficient delivery service to their customers at all times. All the vehicles were maintained and serviced in their own private garage in Roscoe Street, Scarborough.

Now the Natwest Bank on Huntriss Row, originally built by The London & Yorkshire Bank around 1890.

Top of the town centre with the Odeon just visible behind the bus.

Subway Crossing opposite the Odeon believed to have closed in the late 1980's.

A view down the town centre with the Rowntrees department store just visible in the distance.

Harcourt Place viewed from St Nicholas Gardens, demolished in 1899.

Old Scarborough Photo Archive

Mount View Tea Gardens and Cafe in 1912 now known as Back Avenue Victoria.

KINGSCLIFFE HOLIDAY CAMP, SCARBORO'.

Kingscliffe Holiday Camp in the 1920's, now St Nicholas Gardens.

The Albert Hall Liberal Club adjoining the Post Office on
Aberdeen Walk, built in the 1870's.

The Waverley Temperance Hotel, demolished to make way for the Odeon Cinema.

The old court house on Castle Road, built in 1868 and originally
used as the town hall.

North Street, date unknown.

Vernon Place in 1902. The building on the right is now the Three phone shop, the arches still exist but have since been bricked up.

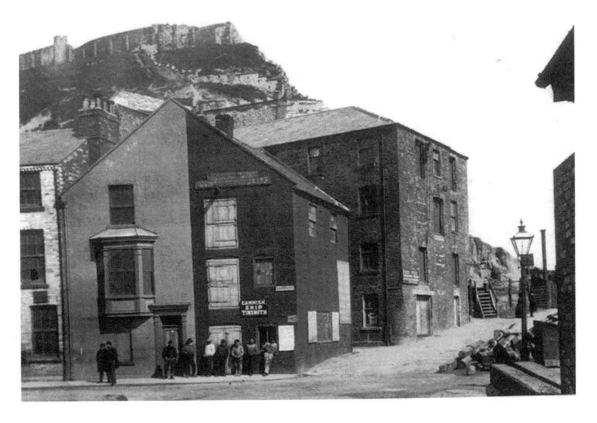

Sandside before the Marine Drive showing the entrance to Quay Street.

A view down Ashville Avenue around 1910.

No3 "Nalgo" Holiday Camp.

Nalgo Holiday Camp in 1931 now Knipe Point.

Construction of the Marine Drive.

Another picture of the construction of the Marine Drive.

Laying the last block of the Marine Drive.

Nesfields Brewery on King Street with barrel kegs outside.

The entrance to Nesfields Brewery on King Street.

In the late 19th and 20th century Scarborough had many breweries such as Nesfields Brewery in King Street, Castle and Phoenix brewery in Castle Road at the top of Auborough Street, another local brewery called the Old Brewery on St Thomas Street which eventually became part of the Scarborough and Whitby Scarborough Brewery Company Limited.

The Scarborough Brewery Company was built in 1850 by Mr Godfrey Knight and was always known as the North Street Brewery.

Godfrey Knight, was the town's Mayor in 1861-63.

The brewery was always kept spotlessly clean. The bottling department bottled their own beer as well as other well known ales such as Bass, Alsopp and Guinness which they sold in their spirit stores. They also sold cigars, cigarettes and tobacco's too!

In 1880 Mr Knight sold the brewery to George and Herbert Hudson, 15 years later they then sold it on in July 1895 and it became known as The Scarborough Brewery Company and it was converted to a limited liability business.

Within two years, a local Whitby brewery had been acquired, and the company was then known as the Scarborough and Whitby Breweries.

Bandstand above the spa pump room, built in 1875 and demolished in 1931.

North Street leading from Castle Road to Newborough.

A view looking up St Thomas Street from St Nicholas Street.

Lower Prospect Road, date unknown.

A row of shops in Princess Square.

Columbus Ravine in 1904.

Back of the police station on Barwick Street looking towards Hanover Road.

Northway in 1957 before redevelopment.

A view down St Thomas Street with Walkers Studios on the left.

Clearing up after the storm in 1953.

Scarborough Coastguard Station after the German bombardment
on 16th December 1914.

St Thomas Street in the early 1930's.

Falsgrave with All Saints Church just visible on the left and the
entrance to the goods station on the right.

Falsgrave roundabout removed in 1980's.

Old Scarborough Photo Archive

Burniston Barracks.

Shop on Barwick Terrace/Brook Square burned down during
the filming of Little Voice.

Although this picture is damaged it shows the Raleigh Street residents celebrating the Queen's Silver Jubilee in 1977.

The residents of Dumple Street and the adjoining Batty Alley in 1931.

32 Princess Street (Woodbine House) which was owned by my
Great Grandmother in the mid 1900's.

Snowdrift Laundry on Scalby Road in 1945, demolished in 1993.

A view of Oxford Street, date unknown.

Churches

All Saints Church in Falsgrave.

Bar Congregational Church on the corner of Westborough onto Aberdeen Walk.

Old Scarborough Photo Archive

Ebenezer Church on Longwestgate after burning down in the early 1950's.

St Thomas Church on East Sandgate.

St Mary's Church on Castle Road with the castle visible on the left.

St Andrews Church on Ramshill Road in 1900.

Wesley Church on the corner of Hoxton Road, before being demolished recently.

Holy Trinity Church on Trinity Road in the early 1920's.

Schools

St Martins Grammar School on Ramshill Road in 1923.

Central School on the corner of Melrose Street and Trafalgar Street West, demolished around 1970.

Convent Of The Ladies Of Mary/Lower Graham School on Queen Street.

Queen Margaret's School in 1904.

Scarborough Boys High School now Yorkshire Coast College Westwood
Campus.

Scarborough Girls High School on Trinity Road.

Arundel House School on Arundel Place.

Patterdale School on Belgrave Crescent in 1934.

High Cliff School on Filey Road in the 1920's.

Foreshore & Sandside

Harbour Bar ice cream parlour in Sandside.

The Madhouse in the 1980's in Sandside.

Foreshore Road in 1912.

Oyster Saloon on the Foreshore, owned by Simpson Rawling.

Blands Cliff in 1910 with the swimming bath on the right.

The Foreshore with the cliff lift to town on the right.

Charles Enoch Arcade/Amusements in Sandside.

Harbour Cafe on Sandside after a fire in the 1950's.

The aftermath of the Olympia fire in August 1975.

Two gentlemen looking at what is left after the fire.

Gentlemen's toilets still standing after the fire and still exist today.

Two firemen tackling what is left of the blaze.

What is left of the doors to the cinema after the fire, later demolished.

About The Author

My name is Joshua Fawcett, I am 15 years old and I was diagnosed with Aspergers Syndrome at the age of 4. I have always had a keen interest in the local history of my hometown of Scarborough. I hope you enjoy looking at the photos and information in my book as much as I have enjoyed producing it.

ISBN 978-1-291-83727-8

HOW TO DO NON-VERBAL REASONING
A STEP BY STEP GUIDE

1+

STEP BY STEP NON-VERBAL REASONING

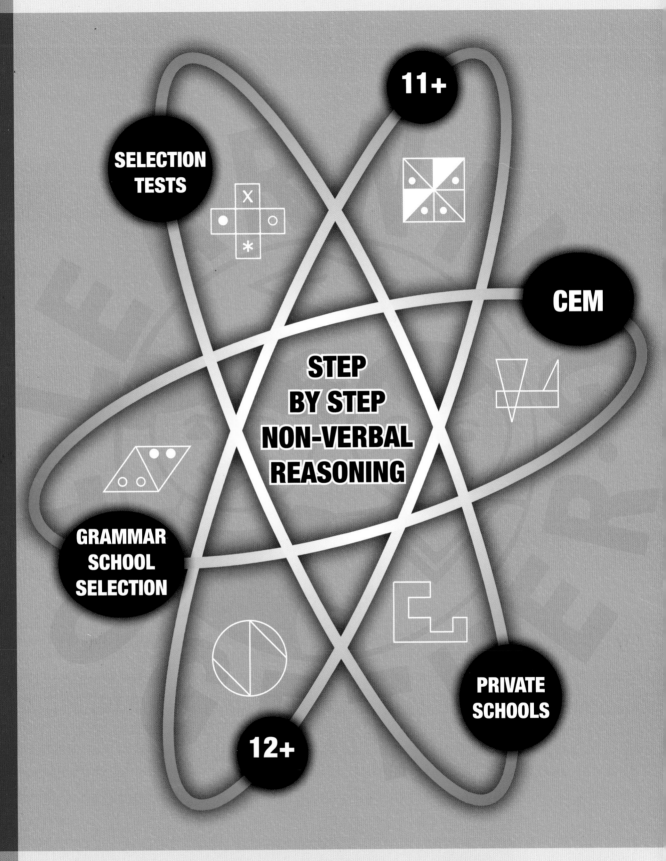

11+

SELECTION TESTS

CEM

STEP BY STEP NON-VERBAL REASONING

GRAMMAR SCHOOL SELECTION

PRIVATE SCHOOLS

12+

**Non Verbal Reasoning Prep suitable for 11+ Selection
Grammar School Selection, School Scholarship
Independent and Private School Selection
By Philip Kay**

Step
y Step
n-Verbal
Book

This book has been written by Philip Kay, an experienced eleven plus tutor who has used this method for many years to explain Non-Verbal Reasoning questions to his pupils. This book is an excellent aid in preparing children for their 11+ or 12+ examinations.

It can also be used in preparing children for grammar school, independent and private school selection tests.

(These tests vary depending on the Local Education Authority or school. You should check requirements with your Local Education Authority or school.)

This book explains the concepts in the Learning Together Non-Verbal Reasoning books.
18 different Non-Verbal Reasoning topics are explained in a simple "Step by Step" manner.

- *Each topic is dealt with in a separate unit.*
- *Each unit has two sections:*

1. The INTRODUCTION with a worked Non-Verbal Reasoning example and Step-by-Step instructions.
2. The EXERCISE that follows has Non-Verbal Reasoning questions with some "Hints" for extra help.

A detachable answer sheet and score sheet to monitor progress are provided at the back of this book.
A pupil working through this book will be better prepared to attempt any Non-Verbal Reasoning questions that he or she might be asked to answer as part of any eleven plus examination.

This Step by Step book Non-Verbal Reasoning book compliments the range of Learning Together Non-Verbal Reasoning and Verbal Reasoning books and their Step by Step Verbal Reasoning book.

Revised edition published 2015
ISBN - 1-873385-24-2
ISBN - 13: 978-1-873385-24-1
© Phillip Kay BA

The right of Philip Kay to be identified as the author of this book has been asserted by him in accordance with the Copyright, Designs and Patents Act.

PUBLISHED BY LEARNING TOGETHER 11+ PUBLISHERS Ltd
18 Shandon Park, Belfast, BT5 6NW
Phone/fax 028 90402086 e-mail: smcconkey@learningtogether.co.uk

WEBSITE: www.learningtogether.co.uk
ONLINE PLATFORM: www.onlineelevenplusexams.co.uk

Whilst the content of this book is believed to be true and accurate at the time of going to press, neither the authors nor publishers can accept any legal responsibility or liability for any errors or omissions that may have been made.